# STILL MORE Riddles

compiled by J. Michael Shannon
illustrated by Diana L. Magnuson

created by The Child's World

CHILDRENS PRESS, CHICAGO

**Library of Congress Cataloging in Publication Data**

Shannon, Michael.
  Still more riddles.

  Summary: A collection of riddles grouped under such categories as science fiction, famous people, children, animals, and scary things.
  1. Riddles, Juvenile. [1. Riddles] I. Magnuson, Diana, ill. II. Child's World (Firm) III. Title.
PN6371.5.S533   1986     818'.5402     85-29065
ISBN 0-516-0186

Copyright © 1986 by Regensteiner Publishing Enterprises, Inc.
All rights reserved. Published simultaneously in Canada.
Printed in the United States of America.

    3 4 5 6 7 8 9 10 11 12 R 93 92 91 90 89 88

# TABLE OF CONTENTS

| | |
|---|---|
| Introduction | 4 |
| About Science Fiction | 5 |
| About Science | 7 |
| About Alphabet Letters | 11 |
| About Famous People | 14 |
| About Sports | 17 |
| About Children | 20 |
| About Animals | 22 |
| About Scary Things | 30 |
| Still More Riddles | 32 |

# Introduction

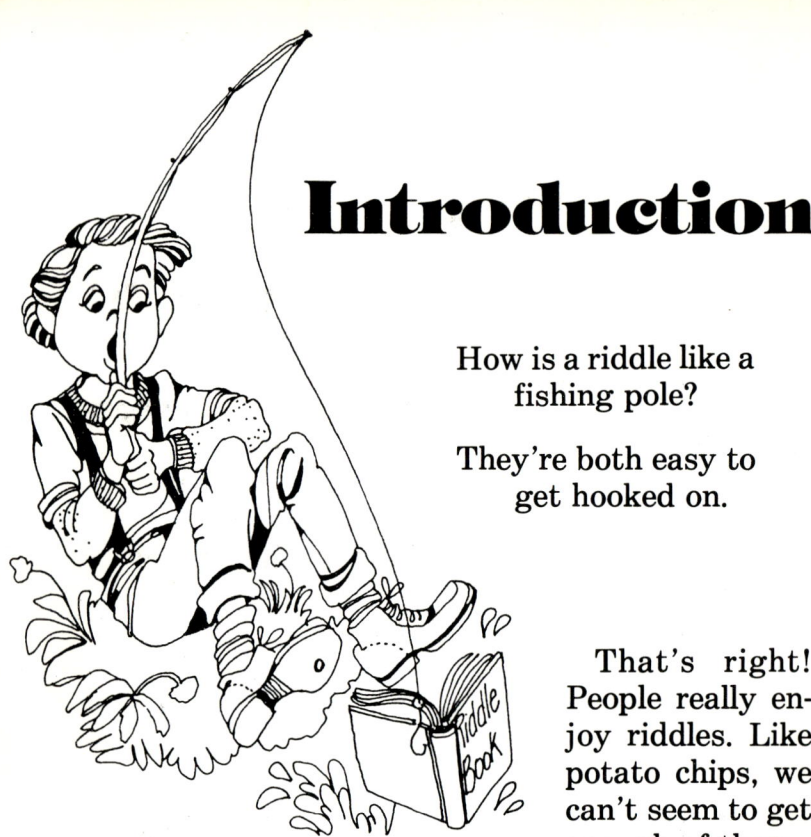

How is a riddle like a fishing pole?

They're both easy to get hooked on.

That's right! People really enjoy riddles. Like potato chips, we can't seem to get enough of them.

Why do people of all ages like riddles? Who knows? We might as well figure out why we laugh or smile. We do know that some riddles make us think. Trying to solve riddles helps us exercise our minds, and that's good. But most of us like riddles because they're clever. . . and they make us laugh. That's good too. We all need some happiness.

So go ahead and enjoy *Still More Riddles*. And go ahead and tell riddles to your friends. But, remember one thing:

When is a riddle like a broken pencil?
When it has no point.

# About Science Fiction

1. Why did the astronaut move to Mars?
2. Why did the boy spell planet P-L-A-N?
3. What dish is out of this world?
4. What Star Trek aliens stick to the wall when you throw them?
5. Why did Spock stop at the Star Ship door?
6. Who is the shortest character in Star Wars?

**ANSWERS:**

1. He heard that living there was out of this world.
2. He heard ET went home.
3. A flying saucer.
4. Klingons.
5. To wait for the Enterprise (enter prize).
6. Han Solo (so low).

7. Do robots like electricity?
8. Where did Luke Skywalker go when he lost his hand?
9. Why did people stay away from the robot?
10. What happened when the robot was struck by lightning?
11. What's big and red and eats rocks?
12. What's big and red and doesn't eat rocks?

**ANSWERS:**

7. Yes, they get a charge out of it.
8. To a second-hand store.
9. He kept flipping his lid.
10. It blew its mind.
11. A big, red rock eater.
12. A big, red rock eater on a diet.

**ST. MARY'S SCHOOL LIBRARY**
**Gilroy, California**

# About Science

1. How do you charge a battery?
2. What kind of water cannot freeze?
3. What is the nastiest fruit?
4. Are mountains conscious of what's going on?
5. What will keep anyone from going bald?
6. Where do atomic scientists go to relax?
7. When is the moon the heaviest?

**ANSWERS:**

1. With a credit card.
2. Hot water.
3. The crab apple.
4. Sure, they have mountain ears (mountaineers) don't they?
5. Hair.
6. They go nuclear fission (fishin').
7. When it is full.

8. What gives bats the energy to fly?
9. Why is it dangerous to let someone cry on your shoulder?
10. What do weather forecasters do when it rains?

11. What goes up when the rain comes down?
12. Why is it dangerous to study flowers?
13. What insects live on the moon?
14. Why did the geologist get fired?
15. Why did the scientist plant a car in the pasture?

**ANSWERS:**

8. Batteries.
9. You might get bacteria (back tear-ia).
10. Get wet.
11. Umbrellas.
12. They all have pistils (pistols).
13. Lunatics (lunar ticks).
14. He began to take all rocks for granite (granted).
15. To see if he could raise a bumper crop.

16. Why are rivers rich in minerals?
17. What works only when it's fired?
18. How do birds grow?
19. Why did the farmer feed dollar bills to his cow?

20. What flowers are on your face?
21. What did one thermometer say to the other?

**ANSWERS:**

16. They have banks on both sides.
17. A rocket.
18. From bird seed.
19. He wanted to get rich milk.
20. Tulips (two lips).
21. "What have you been up to?"

22. What happens when it rains cats and dogs?
23. What is the loudest color?
24. Why does the porcupine seem so upset?
25. Do chickens have a language?
26. What kind of tree can you tell by its bark?
27. What kind of baby gains twenty pounds on elephant's milk?
28. When are false teeth like stars?

**ANSWERS:**

22. You step in puddles.
23. Yeller (yellow).
24. Because he is on pins and needles.
25. Yes, but it's fowl language.
26. A dogwood tree.
27. A baby elephant.
28. When they come out at night.

# About Alphabet Letters

1. What letter can hurt you?
2. What letter can see all?
3. What letter is always surprised?
4. What letter grows in a garden?
5. What letter should always be followed by a question mark?
6. What are the prettiest letters?
7. What are the smelliest letters?
8. What letter do horses eat?
9. What letters are always getting worse and worse?

**ANSWERS:**

1. B (bee)
2. I (eye)
3. O (oh!)
4. P (pea)
5. Y (why)
6. Q-T (cutie)
7. P-U
8. A (hay)
9. D-K (decay)

10. What are the most powerful letters in the alphabet?
11. What letters are like a dried-up well?
12. What letters can people live in?
13. How can you spell mousetrap in three letters?
14. What letters make a bad attitude?
15. What letters can make a number?
16. What letters make a tent?

**ANSWERS:**

10. N-R-G (energy)
11. M-T (empty)
12. C-T (city)
13. C-A-T (cat)
14. N-V (envy)
15. A-T (eighty)
16. T-P (tepee)

17. What letters should you do your best to avoid?
18. What letters grow up a wall?
19. What letters are always cold?
20. What letters are always too much?
21. What letters are always happy?

**ANSWERS:**

17. N-M-E (enemy)
18. I-V (ivy)
19. I-C (icy)
20. X-S (excess)
21. X-T-C (ecstasy)

# About Famous People

1. What do you call Henry Ford's life story?
2. Why did Bob Hope tell jokes to the mirror?
3. Why did Alexander Graham Bell bring a phone to his wedding?
4. Why did Beethoven lead the orchestra?
5. What was Muhammad Ali's least favorite drink?

**ANSWERS:**

1. An auto biography.
2. He thought it might crack up.
3. He wanted a double-ring ceremony.
4. Because they didn't know how to conduct themselves.
5. Punch.

6. What's purple and conquered much of the world?
7. What was Napoleon's favorite tree?
8. How did John Paul Jones stay on his toes?
9. Who was the poorest emperor in Russia?
10. What kind of medicine do you give a sick doll?
11. Which U.S. president was seen in Star Wars?
12. How is an owl like our 16th president?

**ANSWERS:**

6. Alexander the Grape.
7. The infantry (infant tree).
8. By becoming a skipper.
9. Czar Nicholas (nickel less).
10. Dolley Madison (dolly medicine).
11. Ronald Ray gun (Reagan).
12. They're both Abe Lincoln (a blinkin').

13. Why did the sea captain hire Walter Cronkite?
14. Who was the tallest poet?
15. Why did Pete Rose hit the phonograph record with a hammer?
16. Why did people find it hard to trust Michelangelo?

17. How do we know that Adam and Eve were very small?
18. What famous animal needs to be oiled?

**ANSWERS:**

13. He heard Cronkite was an experienced anchor man.
14. Longfellow.
15. He wanted to break a record.
16. Because he was a chiseler.
17. Because they lived in a paradise (pair of dice).
18. Mickey Mouse — he squeaks.

# About Sports

1. How is a baseball team like a pancake?
2. Why did the football team sign two quarterbacks named Ed?
3. Why did the ball park smell bad?
4. What's the best way to hold a bat?
5. Why did the baseball player throw water on home plate?
6. Why did the bowler play so slow?
7. Why did the football team substitute a clock for the football?

**ANSWERS:**

1. They both need a good batter.
2. They heard that two Ed's are better than one.
3. The players hit a lot of foul balls in the stands.
4. By the wings.
5. He wanted to be a clean-up hitter.
6. So he could have time to spare.
7. So they could pass time away.

8. What's the best name for a female tennis player?
9. Did Joseph play tennis in the Bible?
10. Where do Olympic track stars keep their equipment?
11. How do they play basketball in Hawaii?
12. Why did the baseball player wear women's hose?
13. What football player wears the biggest helmet?

**ANSWERS:**

8. Annette.
9. Yes, when he served on Pharoah's court.
10. In a pole vault.
11. With hula hoops.
12. He thought he needed to get more runs.
13. The one with the biggest head.

14. Why did the golfer wear two pairs of pants?
15. What's the difference between a boxer puppy and a professional boxer?
16. Why did the baseball player get sent to jail?
17. What happened to the football player who ran in front of the punter?
18. Why did the runner have to give up his sport?
19. What kind of vehicle does a football team ride in?
20. Why did the baseball player take a rope to the game?

**ANSWERS:**

14. In case he got a hole in one.
15. One weighs a pound and the other pounds away.
16. He stole a lot of bases.
17. He got a kick out of it.
18. He suffered the agony of defeat (da feet).
19. A football coach.
20. In case they needed to tie up the score.

# About Children

1. How is a bad boy like a canoe?
2. Why did the boy bang his head on the piano?
3. What did the shoe say to the boy?
4. Why did the girl fold a dollar bill in half?
5. What did the boy say to the mosquito?
6. Why did the boy tie bananas to his feet?
7. Why did the boy roll up his carpet?
8. Why did the girl sit on her television set?

**ANSWERS:**

1. They both get paddled.
2. He wanted to play by ear.
3. You're putting me on.
4. She wanted to double her money.
5. You get under my skin.
6. He wanted to make a pair of slippers.
7. Because he wanted to see the floor show.
8. She wanted to be on T.V.

9. Why did the girl put clothes on her rabbit?
10. Why did the girl take a ruler to bed?
11. Why did the girl carry a ladder to school?
12. Why did the boy punch a hole in his drum?
13. Why did the boy put his fishing pole in the oven?
14. Why did the girl rip up her homework?
15. Why did the girl tear a page off the calendar?

**ANSWERS:**

9. She wanted to be a hare dresser.
10. So she could see how long she slept.
11. She heard she was moving up to high school.
12. He knew it made it hard to beat.
13. He wanted a hot rod.
14. It was terrible (tear able) work.
15. So she could take a month off.

# About Animals

1. If you put three ducks in a box, what do you get?
2. What's smarter than a talking horse?
3. Why do cows wear bells?
4. How do you catch a unique rabbit?
5. How do you catch a tame rabbit?
6. Why did the cows form a choir?
7. What kind of dog can be grown in a garden?
8. What kind of dog is always lagging behind?
9. What insect knows English?
10. When is a watchdog most likely to enter a house?

**ANIMALS:**

1. A box of quackers.
2. A spelling bee.
3. Because their horns are broken.
4. Unique up on it.
5. Tame way.
6. So they could make beautiful moosic.
7. A collie-flower.
8. A terrier.
9. A spelling bee.
10. When the door is open.

11. Why did the pig put the other animals to sleep?
12. What is the rudest kind of bird?
13. What did the pig say when the farmer cut his tail?
14. Why do ducks have flat feet?
15. Why do elephants have flat feet?
16. What's another name for a dog kennel?
17. What is worse than an elephant with a cold?

**ANSWERS:**

11. He was a boar.
12. A mockingbird.
13. It won't be long now.
14. To stamp out forest fires.
15. To stamp out flaming ducks.
16. A barking lot.
17. A giraffe with a sore throat.

18. What did the bee say to the flower?
19. What did the flower say to the bee?
20. What do birds eat?
21. What do leopards eat?
22. What is the laziest dog?
23. What is the rudest dog?

**ANSWERS:**

18. Hi, Bud!
19. Buzz off.
20. Whatever fits the bill.
21. Whatever hits the spot.
22. The setter.
23. The pointer.

24. What happens if a wolf tries to eat a duck?
25. What do cats sleep on?
26. What do you call the smartest monkey in the tree?
27. How do you pet a porcupine?
28. What did the anteater say to the ant?
29. What could happen if a pig learned karate?

**ANSWERS:**

24. He'll get down in the mouth.
25. A caterpillar.
26. The branch manager.
27. Very carefully.
28. Pleased to eat you.
29. You might get a pork chop.

30. Why was the mother flea so upset?
31. How did the dog get splinters on his tongue?
32. Why was the eagle arrested?
33. Why does a chicken lay eggs?
34. Why do people like parakeets?
35. Why does a flamingo stand on one leg?

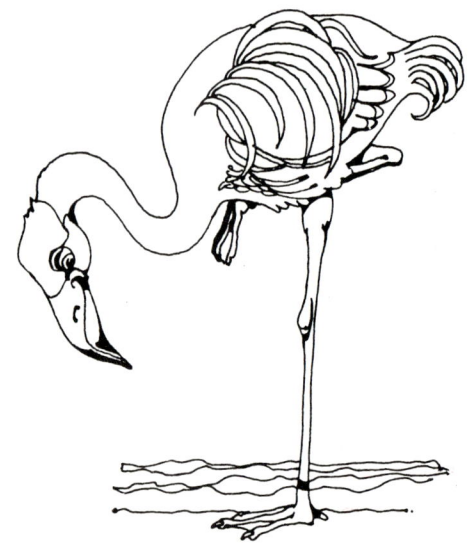

**ANSWERS:**

30. All of her children had gone to the dogs.
31. By eating table scraps.
32. He was an ill eagle.
33. Because if she dropped them, they'd break.
34. Because they make tweet music.
35. Because if he lifted both legs he'd fall.

36. What do criminal sheep do?
37. Where do minnows keep their money?
38. What's another name for a groundhog?
39. What animal is made of wood?
40. Why do giraffes have to be brave?
41. How can you tell when a cow is sad?
42. How do you get rid of bees?
43. What is the heaviest key in the world?

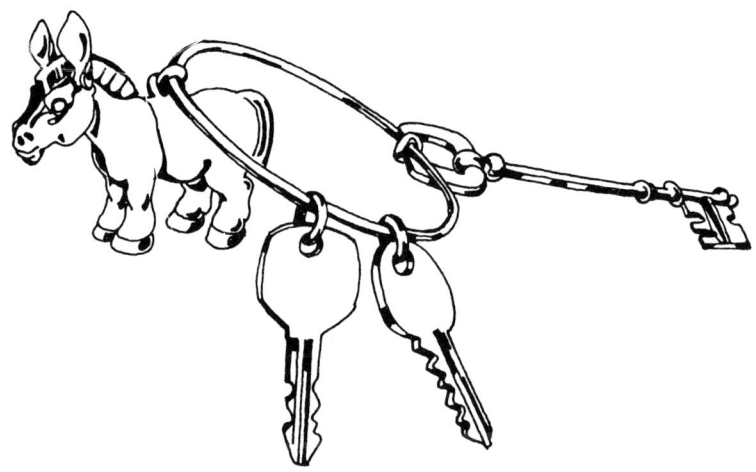

**ANSWERS:**

36. Steel wool.
37. At the river bank.
38. Sausage.
39. The timber wolf.
40. Because they stick their necks out all the time.
41. It gets moo-dy.
42. With a beebee gun (BB gun).
43. A donkey.

44. What is the second heaviest key in the world?
45. What is the third heaviest key in the world?
46. What time is it when an elephant sits on a fence?
47. Where do squirrels store their nuts?
48. How do you get down from an elephant?

**ANSWERS:**

44. A monkey.
45. A turkey.
46. Time to get a new fence.
47. In a branch bank.
48. You don't get down from an elephant. You get down from a duck.

49. What's the best way to talk to a lion?
50. What do you call a pig that crossed the road twice?
51. Why are sheep so poor?
52. What is the most religious insect?
53. What animal is gray and has a trunk?
54. What's as big as an elephant but lighter than a feather?
55. On which side does a duck have the most feathers?

**ANSWERS:**

49. Long distance.
50. A dirty double-crosser.
51. They are always getting fleeced.
52. The praying mantis.
53. A mouse on vacation.
54. An elephant's shadow.
55. The outside.

# About Scary Things

1. Why are ghosts always lonely?
2. What happened to Dracula when he saw the lady vampire?
3. Why does Dracula brush his teeth three times a day?
4. What happened to Dr. Frankenstein's monster when he saw his future bride?
5. How did Dr. Frankenstein cure his loneliness?
6. What should you do to a blue monster?
7. What was Godzilla's favorite meal?
8. Who did Dr. Frankenstein like to spend his time with?

**ANSWERS:**

1. They've got no body.
2. It was love at first bite.
3. So he won't have bat breath.
4. It was love at first fright.
5. He learned how to make friends.
6. Try to cheer him up.
7. Fish and ships.
8. Anyone he could dig up.

9. What did the vampire say to the girl?
10. What's a ghost's favorite sandwich?
11. What should you do if you see a werewolf?
12. Why did the Abominable Snowman paint his head yellow?
13. How do you keep Bigfoot from charging?

**ANSWERS:**

9. You're my type.
10. Boo-logna.
11. Hope he doesn't see you.
12. He wanted to see if blonds had more fun.
13. Take away his credit cards.

# Still More Riddles

1. Why did the seamstress quit her job?
2. Why did the man become a garbage collector?
3. Why did the man quit his job as a garbage collector?
4. Why did the secretary get a tool box?
5. Why did the doctor put his scalpel in the refrigerator?
6. Why did the candlemaker quit her job?

**ANSWERS:**

1. The work was just so so (sew sew).
2. He heard that business was picking up.
3. He was down in the dumps all the time.
4. Her boss told her to file some papers.
5. He wanted to make cold cuts.
6. She didn't want to work on wick ends.

7. Why did the thief carry a bottle of glue?
8. What did the picture say to the wall?
9. What happens to liars when they die?
10. Why did the commentator put a microphone in his mouth?
11. How do students get to Europe?
12. What does a librarian use for bait?
13. What should you do if you find a dragon in your bathtub?
14. Why did the mother kangaroo hate cold, rainy days?

**ANSWERS:**

7. He was planning a stick-up.
8. Help! I've been framed.
9. They lie still.
10. To get the inside story.
11. On scholarships.
12. A bookworm.
13. Pull out the plug.
14. Because the children had to play inside.

15. How do you make a lemon drop?
16. How did the letter get wet in the mail?
17. How did the carpenter lose his teeth?
18. What did one wall say to the other?
19. What did the letter say to the stamp?

**ANSWERS:**

15. Let it fall.
16. It had postage due on it.
17. He got in the habit of chewing his nails.
18. Meet you at the corner.
19. Stick with me, and we'll go places.

20. How do you make a Venetian blind?
21. Why did the lawyer come home early?
22. What kind of cake always tastes bad?
23. What did one elevator say to the other?
24. Why are there fences around graveyards?
25. What did the rabbit say when the fox caught him by the tail?
26. Who always goes to bed with his shoes on?

**ANSWERS:**

20. Poke him in the eye.
21. He had a brief case.
22. A cake of soap.
23. I think I'm coming down with something.
24. People are just dying to get in.
25. That's the end of me.
26. A horse.

27. What did the ground say to the rain?
28. Why did the judge have to give up his job?
29. When is one person like two people?
30. What is the best way to keep milk from getting sour?
31. What did the little hand say to the big hand?

**ANSWERS:**

27. Thanks to you, my name is mud.
28. He had too many trying days.
29. When one is beside oneself.
30. Leave it in the cow.
31. I'll see you in an hour.

32. When is an empty pocket not an empty pocket?
33. Why did the marine get sent home from boot camp?
34. Why did the secretary cut off her fingers?
35. What did one grape say to the other?
36. What question must always be answered "yes"?
37. What stops falling hair?
38. What is an undercover agent?

**ANSWERS:**

32. When there is a hole in it.
33. He was rotten to the corps.
34. So she could write shorthand.
35. I think we're in a real jam this time.
36. The answer is: "How do you say Y-E-S?"
37. The floor.
38. A bedbug.

39. Why is it hard for taxi drivers to make money?
40. Why did the clockmaker quit his job?
41. Why is being a dentist a difficult job?
42. Which hand should you stir soup with?
43. What goes up but never comes down?
44. What kind of coat can only be put on wet?

ANSWERS:

39. They drive their customers away.
40. He got tired of making faces.
41. You often get down in the mouth.
42. Neither. Use a spoon.
43. Your age.
44. A coat of paint.

45. Why was the prisoner glad to get chickenpox?
46. What did the bun say to the hotdog?
47. What's no good until it's broken?
48. Where were the first donuts cooked?
49. What happened when the cook got sick?
50. What did the jack say to the car?

**ANSWERS:**

45. It was his chance for a breakout.
46. Hi, Frank!
47. An egg.
48. In Greece (grease).
49. She couldn't stir for hours.
50. Want a lift?

51. What can you make that no one can see?
52. Why did the gardener quit his job?
53. Why is the sea so romantic?
54. When is a banker like a western hero?
55. What stays in a corner yet travels the world?
56. When is a door not a door?

## ANSWERS:

51. Noise.
52. He was bushed.
53. Because that's where buoy meets gull.
54. When he's a loan arranger (Lone Ranger).
55. A postage stamp.
56. When it's ajar.

57. What goes in the door but never in the house?
58. How many potatoes can be put in an empty bag?
59. How do you stop something from growing?
60. When is corn like a pirate?
61. What's the best day for a parade?
62. Why did the beekeeper quit his job?
63. When is a mountain stream annoying?
64. Why did the tightrope walker carry a calculator with him?

**ANSWERS:**

57. A key.
58. One. After that it's not empty.
59. Rub shortening on it.
60. When it's a buck an ear. (buccaneer).
61. March 4th.
62. The bees gave him the hives.
63. When it is a babbling brook.
64. In case he needed to check his balance.

65. What has no beginning and no end?
66. What does Tarzan sing at Christmas time?
67. Why did the mathematician quit his job?
68. Why did the convict sue the judge?
69. Why did Tarzan get mad at his chimp?
70. Why did the mail carrier quit his job?

**ANSWERS:**

65. A circle.
66. Jungle Bells.
67. He thought his number was up.
68. Because he threw the book at him.
69. He thought he was a cheetah.
70. He lost his zip.

71. What do you call a mixed-up pickle?
72. What do you call a person who really loves chocolate?
73. What is the difference between here and there?
74. Why did the doctor quit his job?
75. Why did the cross-eyed teacher resign?
76. What is the difference between a teacher and a locomotive engineer?

**ANSWERS:**

71. A daffy dill.
72. A cocoa nut.
73. The letter t.
74. He lost his patience (patients).
75. She couldn't control her pupils.
76. One trains the mind, the other minds the train.

77. How do you eat an egg without breaking the shell?
78. What do you call a person who's crazy about money?

79. Why did the knife sharpener quit his job?
80. What's always behind the time?
81. How did gun slingers come to be good artists?

**ANSWERS:**

77. Have someone else break it.
78. A doughnut.
79. He had too much dull work.
80. The back of a clock.
81. They practiced drawing guns every day.

82. What is full of holes yet holds water?
83. What is the difference between a nickel and a penny?
84. What has 100 eyes but no nose?
85. What's purple and hums?
86. What did the balloon say to the pin?

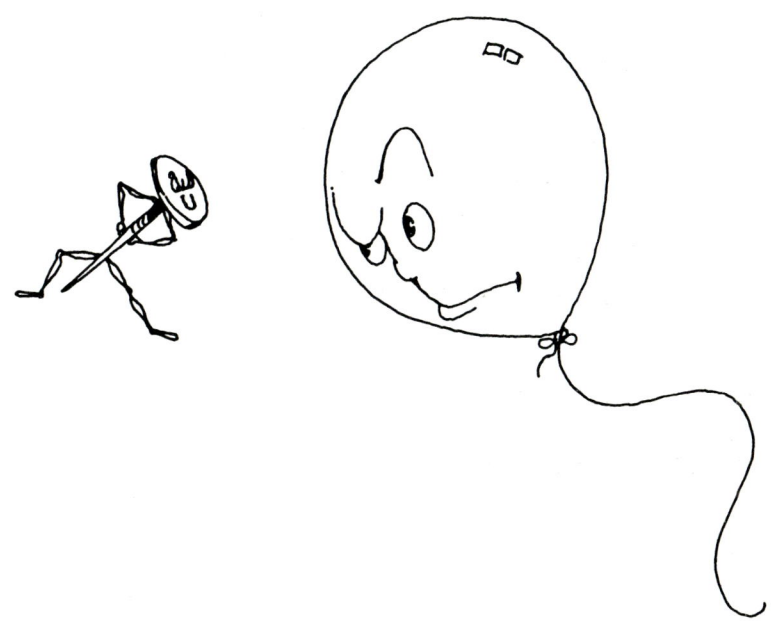

**ANSWERS:**

82. A sponge.
83. Four cents.
84. A bag of potatoes.
85. An electric grape.
86. Stay away from me, buster.

87. Why did Humpty Dumpty have a great fall?
88. What's the first thing you should do every morning?
89. What is the slowest shoe?
90. What is the most mysterious shoe?
91. What is the most dangerous shoe?

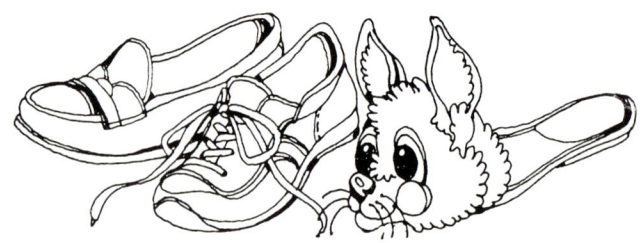

**ANSWERS:**

87. To make up for a bad summer.
88. Wake up.
89. The loafer.
90. The sneaker.
91. The slipper.